A GUIDE ABOUT INVESTING IN GOLD / SILVER

COPYRIGHT 2018 - ALL RIGHTS RESERVED.

This document is geared towards providing exact and reliable information in regards to the topic and issue covered. The publication is sold with the idea that the publisher is not required to render accounting, officially permitted, or otherwise, qualified services. If advice is necessary, legal or professional, a practiced individual in the profession should be ordered.

From a Declaration of Principles which was accepted and approved equally by a Committee of the American Bar Association and a Committee of Publishers and Associations.

In no way is it legal to reproduce, duplicate, or transmit any part of this document in either electronic means or in printed format. Recording of this publication is strictly prohibited and any storage of this document is not allowed unless with written permission from the publisher. All rights reserved.

The information provided herein is stated to be truthful and consistent, in that any liability, in terms of inattention or otherwise, by any usage or abuse of any policies, processes, or directions contained within is the solitary and utter responsibility of the recipient reader. Under no circumstances will any legal responsibility or blame be held against the publisher for any reparation, damages, or monetary loss due to the information herein, either directly or indirectly.

Respective authors own all copyrights not held by the publisher.

The information herein is offered for informational purposes solely, and is universal as so. The presentation of the information is without contract or any type of guarantee assurance.

The trademarks that are used are without any consent, and the publication of the trademark is without permission or backing by the trademark owner. All trademarks and brands within this book are for clarifying purposes only and are the owned by the owners themselves, not affiliated with this document.

Table of Contents

Introduction 1

CHAPTER 1 8

INVESTING IN GOLD & SILVER IS WISE 16

   No Income, No Job, No Assets 16

   Why Gold & Silver 17

   Investing in Gold and Silver 19

   Long Term Strategy 21

   Some History of Gold and Silver Prices 22

   Spikes in Gold and Silver Prices Since 1971 25

   Other Factors Affecting the Price of Gold 26

CHAPTER 2: WHAT ARE PRECIOUS METALS FUTURES CONTRACTS? 30

   Advantages of Futures Contracts 31

   Contract Specifications 32

   Gold 33

   Silver 34

   Hedgers and Speculators 35

HOW TO BUY GOLD AND SILVER 37

   BULLION COINS 37

   ETF 38

   Gold Mining Stocks 39

   Junior Mining Stocks 40

   Commodity Futures 40

Collectible Coins 41
Jewelry 43
Other Comments 44
More on Bullion 46
Preservation of Wealth 46
Tulving.com 47
Traditional Dealer 47
Local Classifieds / Craigs List 48

CHAPTER 3: GOLD AND SILVER BUYING MISTAKES 50
SIMPLE AND SAFE STEPS INVESTING IN GOLD AND SILVER 65

CHAPTER 4 72
CAUTIONS 74
BENEFITS 75
What You Need to Know 76
Housekeeping 77
Why Silver Is a Better Investment Than Gold 78

CHAPTER 5 GOLD VS SILVER 84
GROWING INVESTMENT DEMAND 86
Rising U.S. DEBT 88
THINK AHEAD 89
HISTORY ALWAYS REPEATS 91

THE TWENTY FIRST CENTURY - GOLD AND SILVER BULL MARKET 93

Introduction

The major commercial center linking the Asian kingdoms of the east with the coastal Greek cities of Ionia was Sardis, the capital city of ancient Lydia. So it was only natural that the first coins ever made would start here. Around 650 BC, give or take 10 years either way, coins with the head of a Lion first appeared and was used as the first system of bimetallic currency. These first coins were made of a metal called electrum, an uneven mixture of gold and silver, and sometimes had small traces of copper and or other metals in it.

In Lydia, the most used coins was minted into the weight 4.76 grams, These were called the trites and valued at 1/3rd a stater. Three of these coins weighted about 14.1 grams, and equaled one stater. A stater being about one month's pay for a soldier. One stater size coins as well as smaller fractions were minted also: the trite 1/3rd, the afore mentioned coin, the hekte 1/6th, 1/12th, 1/24th, 1/48th and down to 1/96th of a stater.

It didn't take long for the Greek cities of Ionia to start using electrum to start making their own coins.

Widespread trading of electrum made coins was somewhat hampered however. Because of the uneven mixture of gold and silver, it was rather difficult to determine the exact worth of each coin. For this reason a foreign merchant would offer very low undervalued rates on local electrum coins. In 570 BC pure silver coins were introduced in parts of Greece making these difficulties less and less a problem.

By 560 BC, the Lydians came up with a process to separate the gold from silver, bringing about the minting of the first gold coins. Now gold coins were being produced along with silver coins. Electrum coins did remain a fairly popular form of currency until around 350 BC. Gold and silver coins however quickly became the world standard for currency used in trade. What helped to bring this about so quickly was in 547 BC, when after 13 days of the siege the Persians scaled a lightly defended part of the wall and captured the city of Sardis. Cyrus being amazed with the gold coins found in the Lydian kingdom, decided he wanted to make these gold coins for himself. The Persians learned to mint gold coins and began to use them for trade.

The Greek's liked the use of silver coins as currency and helped to make silver coins excepted as a world standard for currency. Unlike the Greeks, the Persians preferred gold coins over silver, and helped to make gold coins excepted as a world standard for currency. Between the two, gold and silver coins become the money excepted throughout the known world. From that time gold and silver coins has been the only true form of money to this very day.

Sometime in the early 7th century they also become the first to invent paper money. This paper money was called flying money. These first bank notes carried a guarantee that it could be traded at any time for coinage. The paper was not the real money, it was the coinage that it could be traded for that was the real money. The paper was just a form of a promissory note, a promise to trade for real money.

In 1292 when Marco Polo came back from his travels in China telling people about this paper money they used there the people in Europe didn't believe it. It seemed as a joke that the Chinese used paper for money. Paper money in Europe wouldn't come about until the 1600s. In the mid 1600s paper money began to appear throughout Europe, some accepted, some not. The Goldsmithnotes printed by the Bank of England founded in 1694, were again a type of promissory note. These notes were printed as a promise from English gold smiths for account deposits.

The clause "(I) promise to pay the bearer on demand the sum of --- pounds" in gold. Again the paper was not the money, the gold it could be traded in for was the money.

Article 1 section 8 paragraph 5 of The United States Constitution states that Congress has the power "To coin Money, regulate the Value thereof, and of foreign Coin, and fix the Standard of Weights and Measures;"

Article 1 section 10 paragraph 1 of The United States Constitution states that "No State shall ... make any Thing but gold and silver Coin a Tender in Payment of Debts;"

From these 2 sections of The United States Constitution it is clear that our founders did not want paper money as a form of tender in this country, and for good reason. They knew that gold and silver coins have and keep value, and paper always comes to problems. Many of our founders seeing the problems Europe had with their tries at using paper money, plus the early tries of the colonies to use paper money.

In 1836 the first bank notes were printed, with over 30,000 designs and colors, they were easily counterfeited, along with bank failures, became almost as poison to most people. In 1861 Congress authorized the United States Treasury to issue paper money for the first time in the form of non-interest bearing Treasury Notes called Demand Notes. In 1862 these notes were replaced with United States Notes. Commonly called Greenbacks. In 1865 Gold Certificates were issued. In 1868 National Bank Notes, backed by U.S. government securities were printed. In 1878 Silver Certificates in exchange for silver dollars were printed. In 1913 the Federal Reserve Act was passed, then everything changed.

Until this point the paper money printed could be traded in for gold or silver coins - real money. For a while federal reserve notes could be also. From 1913 to 1963 the federal reserve note went from a note that could be traded in for real money to nothing but a piece of paper that is not backed by anything, a debt instrument. Federal reserve notes no longer says it is redeemable for gold or silver, it only says "This Note Is Legal Tender For All Debts Public And Private." In fact the words lawful money is nowhere on the note at all anymore.

Today's federal reserve note is what is called fiat currency. Fiat currency does not have any intrinsic value or any guarantee that it can be converted into gold or another currency. Fiat currency is nothing but a government's order (fiat) that it must be accepted as a means of payment, back by nothing at all. The founders of the United States knew that is what would happen if paper money became accepted. That is why they made gold and silver coins the only form of lawful money in our Constitution.

Paper money never has been and never will be real money. Gold and silver coins has been and still is the only true real money. You hear that gold and silver is going up in value, when in reality it is the paper money going down in value, meaning it takes more paper to buy the same amount of gold. Back when quarters were still made of silver you could buy a loaf of bread with one of them. Today that same quarter made of silver would still buy you a loaf of bread.

Gold and silver coins is the safest place to invest your paper dollars. It is the one thing you can invest in that will never go broke. Stocks and bonds may crash, paper money may become worthless, banks may fail, but all through history gold and silver retains value. It is well known that Gold coins are the safest and most risk free place to invest ones savings. As the news informs us of the failing economy, and we see prices of everything go through the roof we need to find a safe place to put our hard earned federal reserve notes. At the decay rate of the dollar, if you can survive on $20.000.00 a year today, in about 10 years it will take you over $50,000.00 a year to live the same life style. That same $20,000.00 in gold coins in 10 years will last longer than a year.

Paper currencies offer you no protection in your investments, it only loses more and more value with each passing year. There is nothing that offsets the shrinking value of currencies like gold coins. When you save gold and silver bullion coins, such as the American Eagles, you build yourself a fortress of investment security.

CHAPTER 1

Since prehistoric man first stumbled upon a nugget, raw gold with its radiant sun yellow coloration and metallic luster has captivated and fascinated mankind. The unique gleam of gold attracts the eye, enabling the seeker to detect the smallest of grains in an aggregate of many other materials. The tiniest flakes are easily detected.

Anthropological excavations of Stone Age burial sites indicate that gold was the first element collected and prized by man. This unique metal, gathered in the form of nuggets, seems to have been highly prized but was not used in practical applications. Rating 2.5 - 3 on Mohs scale of hardness, gold was much too pliable to be hammered into workable tools or weapons. Gold carried little value for prehistoric man except to be admired and treasured for its rare, intrinsic beauty. However, as man developed he soon discovered numerous applications for the mysterious golden metal.

The earliest record of gold exploration dates to Egypt around 2000 B.C. Ancient records tell of an enormous alluvial gold deposit in Nubia, between the Nile River and the Red Sea in southeastern Egypt. This incredible discovery encompassed over one hundred square miles. Using the most primitive of tools and working to an average depth of less than six feet, these first "miners" pried an estimated one thousand tons of gold from this rich discovery. Egyptian artisans, recognizing the extraordinary malleability of gold fashioned incredible jewelry, ornaments and idols of breathtaking beauty.

Throughout the history of man's involvement with gold, the precious metal has been prized not only for its beauty but for gold's ability to withstand the rigors of time. No substance that appears commonly in nature will destroy gold. Unaffected by air, moisture, heat or cold, this noble metal will not tarnish, corrode, rust or tarnish. Shimmering gold dust, golden nuggets of placer gold and brilliant vein occurrences have survived 4.5 Billion years of cataclysmic geologic and climate changes; volcanic eruption, earthquakes, upheavals and deposition. Treasures of gold jewelry, bullion and coins, buried for thousands of years beneath land and sea have been found intact; as brilliant as the day they were abandoned.

A relatively rare native metallic element, gold ranks fifty-eighth in abundance amongst the ninety two natural elements that make up the earth's crust. Although considered a rare element, of all metals gold is, with the exception of iron, the most widely distributed over the planet. Gold has been found on 90 per cent of the earth's surface and is mined in high mountain ranges, in the deeply weathered soil of the tropics, harsh deserts and in the permanently frozen tundra of the Arctic.

Gold is commercially mined on every continent with the exception of Antarctica. The richest gold producing area of the world is the Witwatersrand District of South Africa. This ultra rich area has yielded eighteen thousand tons of gold with no end in sight. Additional notable gold bearing areas around the world are Siberia in the former USSR, the Porcupine District in Ontario, Canada and in the United States the Yukon District of Alaska and the famous Mother Lode District in California.

In the United States nature was extremely generous. Thirty-two states have recorded significant commercial gold production. The highest yielding areas are located within the western states, California, Colorado, Alaska,

Nevada and South Dakota. Other abundant locations for prospecting include Georgia, Arkansas, Idaho, Utah, Montana, Washington, New Mexico, Wyoming, North and South Carolina, Tennessee, Michigan, Vermont and New Hampshire. The recreational gold prospector can find gold in his pan in practically every state of the union.

Gold is an exceptional media for craftsmen. Gold is a metal that can be deformed by pounding without breaking or crumbling. Gold, in its pure form is the most malleable or workable of all metals. One single ounce of gold can be drawn and stretched into an ultra fine wire over 50 miles in length without breaking or pounded to the amazing thinness of one hundred thousandth of an inch without disintegrating. Gold is easily carved, readily buffs to a gleaming polish, can be heated repeatedly without discoloration and joins to itself or other metals by soldering without the need for a bonding flux.

For more than 6000 years gold has been considered symbolic of wealth, power and status. In 1350 B.C. the Egyptian boy king, Tutankhem, was interred in a coffin elaborately cast from 242 pounds of solid gold. Throughout history men and women have adorned their bodies with brilliant, gleaming gold. The ancient custom of exchanging gold during marriage ceremonies continues today.

The nobility of Medieval Europe liberally sprinkled gold in the form of dust, flake or leaves on their food to demonstrate the host's great wealth. Today gold is still often used in food and has the E Number 175. However, since metallic gold is inert to all body chemistry, it adds no taste nor has any other nutritional effect and leaves the body unaltered. Primitive man believed gold contained a hidden, internal fire, a gift from the Gods with mysterious healing and magical powers. Numerous cultures of sun-worshippers revered gold as the tangible essence of their God; solid sunshine. In modern day Japan believers seek gold's medicinal magic by immersion in a bathtub designed in the form of a phoenix crafted from 400 pounds of pure gold. Health and gold have long been entwined in the wondrous belief that something so rare and beautiful could not be anything but healing and healthy.

Today modern esotericists and forms of alternative medicine embrace the healing properties of gold. Some gold salts have anti-inflammatory properties and are used as pharmaceuticals in the treatment of arthritis and other similar conditions. However, only salts and radioisotopes of gold are of pharmacological value, as elemental or metallic gold is inert to all chemicals it encounters within the body.

Gold is a "storehouse of value", the natural way for man to preserve capital and protect against financial uncertainty or monetary collapse. In modern times gold has served as a hedge against the threat of inflation and as a secure and safe way to secret away assets. The "hoarding" of gold occurs most frequently during times of war, adverse world conditions and international fears of economic instability. Gold has often defeated the attempts of governments to inflate the currency of their country as well as circumventing the aims of those holding political power to direct the economy of other nations.

Throughout recorded history, gold, the crowned king of metals, has been considered the ultimate monetary exchange. Gold is the only currency that isn't someone else's responsibility or liability; it is more that just a paper promise to pay upon demand. Gold's worth does not rely on the economic stability of any country, political power or financial cartel. Gold has value in and of itself.

The current world price of gold is established daily by the London Gold Market which trades gold bullion and coins with other financial world centers such as Zurich, Hong Kong , Frankfurt and Paris. The price is based on pure or "fine" gold, therefore the value of gold gleaned in its natural state may vary depending on the impurities it contains. However, raw gold sold as specimens or jewelry will always bring a considerably higher price. Gold nuggets are as distinctively different as snowflakes, although similar, no two nuggets are alike. A nugget of unique character and shape may sell for as much as five times its value by weight.

Do you have broken or discarded gold jewelry you not longer wear? Now may be the time to cash in on the current gold rush. With the price of gold exceeding the $1000 an ounce benchmark, an errant earring or broken gold chain could add up to a significant sum.

To receive the best price for gold you may wish to sell, know the karat count. Because of the softness of pure 24k gold, it is usually alloyed with base metals for use in jewelry, altering its hardness, color, melting point and ductility. Alloys with lower karatage, typically 22k, 18k, 14k or 10k, contain higher percentages of silver, copper or other base metals in the alloy. The higher the karat the more you should expect to be paid.

If you only have a piece or two to sell, try a local jeweler or take a vintage piece to an antique jeweler. They'll take the artist's craftsmanship into consideration and you will net a much higher price than for just the gold weight.

Nandu Green is a lifestyle portal, offering high-quality, unique, intriguing and innovative merchandise from around the globe.

INVESTING IN GOLD & SILVER IS WISE

No Income, No Job, No Assets

This is the mantra for a new generation, a generation of people who are at their wits end when it comes to feeling like the percent of people that don't have a voice or a way out. The way in which the world manages finances is about to change the way people view all the things they have been taught by their parents. The days of get a job with a good company and invest in a 401k are pretty much gone. That money will not be enough with prices increasing the way they are.

Most can not even land a solid job. Yes they have a college degree and a mountain of debt which they are now finding was a big mistake. The N.I.N.J.A generation stands for No Job, No Income and No Assets. My job is to help this generation of people secure income and assets so they can transform their lives for the future and a great way to accumulate assets with little money is in Gold and Silver Investing.

Why Gold & Silver

Gold and Silver are known as precious metals. These metals come from the earth and can not be recreated my man which is what makes it valuable. You may recognize Gold and Silver as the basic material for most jewelry on the market but there are other uses for these precious metals. For instance silver is used in almost all electronic items due to its high conductivity (ability to transfer an electrical signal). That includes every thing from the satellites that orbit the earth down to the cell phone you use. Gold is used in areas where corrosion can occur but must truly be avoided.

Gold and Silver have also been used for currencies for centuries. We can date this back way before the Roman Empire but will use them in the illustrations so that we can understanding the significance of the metals. We have all heard of the great Roman Empire that eventually fell underneath its own weight. Well the Roman Empire used a currency to trade with surrounding nations and to pay taxes. Paying taxes is what allows the government to finance wars and pay civil service employees. After a while Rome began to expand its reach by conquering nearby areas and going to war with other countries. This war was fueled by the items that needed money and the major form of currency was silver and gold.

Well as Rome began to expand it took on more debt, more service members where employed than ever and there were more projects being taken on than the government could handle in the end. Julius Caesar notice the Roman empire began pulling back in spending. This would be later known as a recession, very similar to what is going on around the world as of 2012. Since Gold was the standard for trade among the town and was used to pay taxes the government had to find a way to increase the amount of gold to stimulate the economy. This is what we call Quantitative Easing in the U.S. Since gold is a natural resource from the earth they devised a way to cut corners off the gold coins so that they had a lower per ounce gold amount. This devaluing of the gold coin (similar to a quarter) caused prices to increase steadily.

As time went on prices increased as more of these corner clipped coins entered society. Eventually the government could not clip the corners anymore than they already had so the began mixing the gold with another metal so there were more coins (quarters) in circulation but there value was a lot less than the original

100% Gold coin. Eventually Rome experienced hyperinflation and the empire was destroyed.

Am tell you this story because we face the same scenario today and will help you understand the need for holding precious metals like gold and silver. We have now evolved from the use of gold to the use of paper dollars across the world. Those dollars where once redeemable for gold.

Yes! The U.S dollar was once backed by gold and was as good as gold. President Nixon made Julius Caesar decision and decided to begin cutting corners and eventually took the nation off of the Gold Standard.

Gold Standard - when a monetary system bases it currency against a certain amount of Gold. Ex. $20 bill = 1 ounce of gold.

Investing in Gold and Silver

In the N.I.N.J.A era, holding assets will become the way we keep any money or wealth. Theses assets can be anything from a business to real-estate or precious metals. An asset is simply any item that produces income or preserves wealth. Now you do not have to be rich to be involved with any of these assets in fact more people have gotten involved with these asset classes from middle income homes that ever before. We want to focus on investing in silver and gold as a means for storing wealth. As median income earners it is very difficult for us to sometimes save money are we may feel that saving money is a useless event.

Investing in Gold and Silver can be quite exciting. It gives financially astute people the benefit of holding some physical wealth and for those who just have a joy in purchasing things it allows you to shop around and buy bargain metals. Yes, I know it doesn't sound all that sexy but either way silver and gold were used in the roman empire and are still being used today. Countries use it to buy oil and other imports from other countries.

Gold and Silver are important because not matter how much prices fluctuate gold and silver will buy the same amount of that item at anytime. For instance 1 ounce of Gold bought a Roman Soldier a tailored war suit, belt, durable shoes and a few accessories. Today 1 ounce of gold will buy a well tailored suit, a nice belt, some fine shoes and a few accessories. The price of the suites in relative terms have increased but it still maintains its weight in gold and that what we need to understand.

Gold and Silver Performance

February 2007: $665/ ounce

February 2008: $974/ ounce

February 2009: $995/ ounce

February 2010: $1,141/ ounce

February 2011: $1,418/ ounce

February 2012: $1,649/ ounce

That is a 148% Return on your first investment in 6 years. It also means that the value of U.S dollars against Gold is decreasing by 17% annually. Remember 1 ounce will always buy you the same item so that means the value of the dollar is decreasing by 17% when on the dollar.

Long Term Strategy

Build up your assets so you can keep wealth in both good and bad times. Purchasing a little gold and silver over time will help you feel secure about your future and promote regular savings. I want you to be aware that gold and silver are not so much investment vehicles that pay out income. Yes you may be able to sell it for more than you paid for it but does not mean that it made you any real money it only preserves the value. You can use ETF's and Futures contracts to make income while still holding physical precious metals. I teach more about these strategies in my book and courses.

Some History of Gold and Silver Prices

From 1792 to 1933, the gold price was $20.67 per ounce in the United States - all money could be exchanged for gold. In 1933, the US went off this gold standard, devalued the dollar to $35 per ounce of Gold, and forbade any US citizen from holding or owning any gold. Foreign citizens and banks could, however, convert their US notes into gold. After World War II, the gold-backed US dollar became the world's key currency for several reasons:

- The European countries involved in WWII were heavily in debt to the US.

- The US economy was very strong and the value of dollar had appreciated.

- Of all the major world currencies, only the US dollar was backed by gold.

- The US agreed to link the dollar to the gold price of $35 per ounce and exchange gold bullion for dollars.

In 1971, the dollar became fiat money; the dollar became merely a paper note having neither value in itself nor backing in real assets. This happened when President Nixon ended the ability of foreign banks to convert their US dollars into gold. Nixon's action eliminated the official $35 per ounce price of gold - the value of gold and the value of the dollar were no longer linked.

The private market, which in 1968 was allowed to set a separate price for gold, then determined the world's only gold price. At the time of Nixon's order, the gold price had recently risen to about $40 per ounce and the silver price was about $1.40 per ounce. (The market quoted gold and silver prices in US dollars per ounce.)

Since 1971, the value of the fiat dollar lay in the US government's declaration that the dollar is legal money to exchange for goods and services. The US Treasury could then pay its bills and its debts in fiat dollars. Standing behind the national debt has been the increasingly shaky assurance that the US government, or rather the US taxpayer, is good for every dollar that is owed. Still, for almost 40 years, the dollar has remained the world's currency standard largely because of the past strength and continuing importance of the US economy.

After the dollar had become fiat money, gold and silver prices increased modestly at first. But by the end of 1974, when the right of US citizens to own gold was finally restored, the price of gold had risen above $180 per ounce and the price of silver above $4.00 per ounce.

As precious metals and former currency standards, gold and silver prices almost always rise and fall together. What factors affect their price? Is now the time to make a profitable gold or a silver investment?

Yes, now is a great time for a gold or silver investment. The US and the world are on the brink of changes that could heighten economic uncertainty, and even produce fear. Of course, no one can predict any future price, but such uncertainty increases the demand for gold and silver and drives their prices up.

Spikes in Gold and Silver Prices Since 1971

Unusual or extreme conditions existed during three times when the price of gold and silver rose abnormally high. These factors often accompany economic uncertainty and higher gold prices.

1973-1975: Troubling the nation and world were the Watergate scandal, President Nixon's resignation, and Arab members taking control of OPEC and cutting oil production. Inflation was high and spiked to over 12%. The rise in the gold coincided with consumer confidence plummeting to an historic low. Additionally, gold climbed and fell nearly in tandem with both inflation and the unemployment rate, which reached 9%. Interest rates also surged to a post-war high of 12% just months before gold peaked at nearly $200 an ounce.

All of 1980: This was the year of the Iran hostage crisis. Gold and interest rates were both extremely high and extremely volatile. The price of gold skyrocketed to $850 per ounce, dropped to $485, and surged again to $710 before dropping again. Interest rates followed gold by a few months in rising to 20%, falling to 11%, and climbing back to

21% by year's end. Consumer confidence plunged briefly and the inflation rate grew to over 14%; it was higher than 11% for nearly two years.

1982,83: Consumer confidence was very low for a prolonged period, likely caused by the highest unemployment rates since the great depression and a very high interest rates, still over 16% when gold began its rise from $296 per ounce. Inflation, however, had dropped below 7% and continued to drop as the gold price stayed between $395 and $510 per ounce.

Other Factors Affecting the Price of Gold

Deficit Spending:

Long term budget deficits decrease a country's economic stability.

Debasing the Currency:

When a nation borrows money or increases its (fiat) money supply by printing, the value of its currency decreases. Gold, however, maintains its value. Thus, when the dollar loses value, the price of gold generally increases and vice versa.

Uncertain Conditions Today:

From 1988 through the end of 2001, through the market crash of 2000 and even 9/11, the price of gradually gold fell while the dollar's value was erratic until 1995 when it increased dramatically. Unemployment, inflation, and interest rates were all low and produced the feeling of economic stability.

In January 2002, the price of gold began its rise from $280 per ounce to over $900 per ounce in 2008. During that time, the inflation rate, the interest rate, and the unemployment rate all remained low, while deficit spending and borrowing increased. Uncertainty began to build because of the wars in Afghanistan and Iraq. Gold prices seemed to rise and fall with the conditions in the Middle East, rising with the deterioration in 2006 & 2007 and falling in 2008 with the improvement in Iraq.

Dire economic conditions built up across the globe throughout 2008 and gold began a steep rise to its current price near $1200 per ounce. There are many reasons for that. Unemployment rose and stayed high. Deficit spending, debt, and money supply increases hurt currencies and economies. While gold prices are most affected by the stability of the US economy, deep weaknesses in the Euro and in many European economies have contributed to the current uncertainty.

Unfortunately, the economic uncertainty is likely to increase and put even more upward pressure on gold and silver prices. A gold investment or a silver investment could now be highly profitable for several reasons.

- Inflation remains low. Its rise will lower purchasing power and trouble businesses and consumers.
- Interest rates remain low. Its rise will produce many new economic problems.
- Debt and deficit spending are projected to remain very high. Paper fiat money will be worth less and less.
- The dollar has strengthened along with the recent rise in the gold price as Euros are being converted into

both dollars and gold. Is this temporary or artificial? Will the dollar fall in value?

- Disruptive terror attacks loom. God forbid that a serious attack is successful.

- Nuclear aspirations of Iran and North Korea are troubling.

- The Middle East seems closer to war than to peace.

Of course, none of these events are desired. Yet, with eyes open, the wise person will be prepared and the wise investor will seriously consider purchasing gold and silver.

CHAPTER 2:
WHAT ARE PRECIOUS METALS FUTURES CONTRACTS?

A precious metals futures contract is a legally binding agreement for delivery of gold or silver in the future at an agreed upon price. The contracts are standardized by a futures exchange as to quantity, quality, time and place of delivery. Only the price is variable.

Hedgers use these contracts as a way to manage their price risk on an expected purchase or sale of the physical metal. It also provides speculators with an opportunity to participate in the markets without any physical backing.

There are two different positions one can take in the markets. A long position is an obligation to accept delivery of the physical metal, and a short (sell) position is the obligation to make delivery. The great majority of futures contracts are offset prior to the delivery date. For example, this occurs when an investor with a long position initiates a short position in the same contract, effectively eliminating the original long position.

Advantages of Futures Contracts

Because they trade at centralized exchanges, trading futures contracts offers more financial leverage, flexibility and financial integrity than trading the commodities themselves.

Financial leverage is the ability to trade and manage a high market value product with a fraction of the total value. Trading futures contracts is done with performance margin. It requires considerably less capital than the physical market. The leverage provides speculators a higher risk/higher return investment.

For example, one futures contract for gold controls 100 troy ounces, or one brick of gold. The dollar value of this contract is 100 times the market price for one ounce of gold. If the market is trading at $600/ounce, the value of the contract is $60,000 ($600 x 100 ounces). Based on exchange margin rules, the margin required to control one contract is only $4,050. So for $4,050, one can control $60,000 worth of gold. As an investor, this gives you the ability to leverage $1 to control roughly $15.

In the futures markets, it is just as easy to initiate a short position as a long position, giving participants a great amount of flexibility. This flexibility provides hedgers with an ability to protect their physical positions and for speculators to take positions based on market expectations.

The exchanges in which gold/silver futures are traded offer participants no counter party risks, which are ensured by the clearing services. This means that the exchange acts as a buyer to every seller, and vice versa, decreasing the risks should either party default on their responsibilities.

Contract Specifications

There are a few different gold contracts traded on U.S. exchanges: one at COMEX and two on eCBOT. There is a 100 troy ounce contract that is traded at both exchanges and a mini contract (33.2 troy ounces) traded only at the eCBOT.

Silver also has two contracts trading at the eCBOT and one at the COMEX. The 'big' contract is for 5,000 ounces, which is traded at both exchanges, while the eCBOT has a mini for 1,000 ounces.

Gold

Gold is traded in dollars and cents per ounce. For example, when gold is trading at 600/ounce, the contract has a value of $60,000 (600 x 100 ounces). A trader that is long at 600 and sells at 610 will make $1,000 (610 - 600 = $10 profit, 10 x 100 ounces = $1,000). Conversely, a trader who is long at 600 and sells at 590 will lose $1,000.

The minimum price movement or tick size is $0.10. The market may have a wide range, but it must move in increments of at least $0.10.

Both the eCBOT and COMEX specify delivery to New York area vaults.

These vaults are subject to change by the exchange.

The most active months traded (according to volume and open interest) are February, April, June, August, October and December.

To maintain an orderly market, the exchanges will set position limits. A position limit is the maximum number of contracts a single participant can hold. There are different position limits for hedgers and speculators.

Silver

Silver is traded in dollars and cents per ounce like gold. For example, if silver is trading at $10/ounce, the 'big' contract has a value of $50,000 (5,000 ounces x $10/ounce), while the mini would be $10,000 (1,000 ounces x $10/ounce).

The tick size is $0.001 per ounce, which equates to $5 per big contract and $1 for the mini contract. The market may not trade in a smaller increment, but it can trade larger multiples, like pennies.

Like gold, the delivery requirements for both exchanges specify vaults in the New York area.

The most active months for delivery (according to volume and open interests) are March, May, July, September and December.

Silver, like gold, also has position limits set by the exchanges.

Hedgers and Speculators

The primary function of any futures market is to provide a centralized marketplace for those who have an interest in buying or selling physical commodities at some time in the future. The metal futures market helps hedgers reduce the risk associated with adverse price movements in the cash market. Examples of hedgers include bank vaults, mines, manufacturers and jewelers.

Hedgers take a position in the market that is the opposite of their physical position. Due to the price correlation between futures and the spot market, a gain in one market can offset the losses in the other. For example, a jeweler who is fearful that she will pay higher prices for gold or silver would then buy a contract to lock in a guaranteed price. If the market price for gold/silver goes up, she will have to pay higher prices for gold/silver. However, because the jeweler took a long position in the futures markets, she could have made money on the futures contract, which would offset the increase in the cost of purchasing the gold/silver. If the cash price for gold/silver and the futures prices both went down, the hedger would lose on her futures positions, but pay less when buying her gold/silver in the cash market.

Unlike hedgers, speculators have no interest in taking delivery, but instead try to profit by assuming market risk. Speculators include individual investors, hedge funds or CTAs (commodity trading advisers).

Speculators come in all shapes and sizes and can be in the market for different periods of time. Those who are in and out of the market frequently in a session are called scalpers. A day trader holds a position for longer than a scalper, but usually not overnight. A positions trader holds for multiple sessions. All speculators need to be aware that if a market moves in the opposite direction, their position can results in losses.

HOW TO BUY GOLD AND SILVER

BULLION COINS

This is my preferred choice for current times. Commission costs are small. Common bullion coins are easily sold, often to dealers or even via local classifieds or Craigslist. But where you buy matters. Prices can vary from dealer to dealer by as much as 5% or even more. You will generally have to pay in cash (if local) or wire transfer. For any dealer giving you competitive pricing, the cost of credit card processing is just too high. If your dealer takes credit cards, you are WAY Overpaying. More on sources at the end of this article. Storage can become an issue if you are buying large quantities. But in the case of gold, 100 coins (or five rolls of 20) is a small little package (maybe 8x1.5x2 inches) and has a value of $135,000 or so. Easy enough to hide in a sock drawer. A case of silver Eagles (500, or 25x20 coins) is bigger (10x10x2 inches?) and only stores $15,000 of wealth. Even 10 cases (5000) of silver coins is not THAT big, but is noticeable.

You could put them in a safe deposit box, and that is the traditional suggestion. But you may be running some additional risk of confiscation (more on this later).

ETF

ETF's are liquid. You can buy and sell them in seconds inside any stock brokerage account. But they have some drawbacks. Biggest is taxes.

Unlike a regular ETF, precious metals ETFs are treated differently by the IRS, and you will have to pay income taxes each year whether you sell them or not. Additionally, they are treated as regular income, not capital gains, so you pay a much higher rate. Before you buy any ETF's, speak with a tax advisor to determine which rules affect you and whether they have been changed since I last checked them.

Gold ETF's have some special concerns. There have been rumors for years that the GLD is not holding as much gold as they are supposed to have. Can you spell "fraud"? Even more disturbing, the gold ETFs were growing so fast a few years ago that they did not have time to verify what they were buying. Stories of them buying gold-plated tungsten abound, and again this will not become obvious until they try to sell this stuff. Even more scary yet, GLD does not have to hold gold at all. They can have your money invested in "gold investments", which basically means derivatives, options, and futures contracts. If you want to own gold and silver as protection against a financial collapse, GLD and their cousins will be the first ones to fail in a market meltdown. ETFs may sound good in theory, but they do not provide the protection you should be seeking. Run Away.

Gold Mining Stocks

Owning some mining stocks may be a good idea. They provide some protection against outright confiscation, since you know that they will be exempted. But the companies themselves can be nationalized, or individual mines can be taken. So you have to look at WHERE the company has it's mines and be aware of political risk. In addition, you are buying a company, so have all the risks and challenges that entails.

Lower earnings. Fraud (ala ENron). Rising costs. Bad management. Hedging programs can make companies insensitive to the price of gold, so buying a gold miner may not give you the appreciation you expect. And watch out for leverage - mining stocks tend to move faster than the metal, up AND down. They are not bad investments, but you have to do your homework and you have to understand exactly what you are buying.

Junior Mining Stocks

Junior Mining Stocks have the all the drawbacks of senior mining stocks. Plus they are VERY speculative. They may or may not have any proven reserves. They might not own a single truck or hard hat or single ounce of gold. Even in good times they trade based on rumors and gossip. As a group, they are one of the most fraud-ridden areas of the stock market. And they are not for casual or even most professional investors. Be especially careful of junior miners that do not trade on a U.S. exchange. But the best advice is just do not mess with them at all. You can have more fun losing your money in Las Vegas, and at least they will comp you a cheap buffet meal.

Commodity Futures

Not for the timid. This is the "market", where price discovery happens and where all other gold pricing is based. To trade in it, you just need to open a commodities account. The big risk is leverage. You can buy a single gold futures contract with about $3800, and you control 100 ounces of gold. That means you have about 3% of the contact value amount. If gold goes up by $38 an ounce, you have doubled your money. If it goes down by $38 you are wiped out. And believe me, gold can move a lot more than $38 in a single hour during a selloff or panic. It is a good market, and reasonably fair, but you REALLY need to have some sophistication to play here. Not for the neophyte.

Collectible Coins

Coins are pretty. They are fun to look at and to collect. Prices can vary way more than bullion coins. The same coin might be listed in a coin price list as valued at $100, but be available for $50 or $125. They always trade a significant premium to melt value, yet the sellers mention "melt" quite often when trying to convince you they are good investments. It's true that a collectible coin will always be worth at least melt (well almost always). But the value may have to double just to break even. When I make an investment, I don't want to wait for it to double just to break even. In addition, when you want to sell a collectible, you have to go to a dealer or find another collector in order to get some part of your premium. Dealers typically work on a 25-50% markup, so that $100 coin that a dealer is selling at $50 might only be worth $30 when you are ready to sell it.

This is a very specialized area. People who are serious about coins live and breathe them. There is no logic, it is completely about special cases. One year can be worth 1000 times another one, and the only way to know is to know. Catalog prices are at best a general guide, but not very useful. Unless you want to become serious about this market and learning about it (10-20 hours a week for a year might get you started, for 20 years is better), my advice is to stay away as an investment.

But coins are pretty. Buy some if you like to look at them, as they certainly are better than most artwork. They make great gifts, especially for children. If you are a silver buyer, there is something special about having a complete set of American Silver Eagles in MS-69 grade. As bullion, you could buy these 26 coins today for about $860. As collectible certified coins, one company is offering this exact collection for $1450. right now. Or maybe you want a nice collection of coins from the various countries. Some are very beautiful as art. These are pretty and nice to show off to your friends, and bullion is NOT. But for real save-your-ass investing, stick with bullion. The coin collection goes to your grandchildren in your will, so you don't have to know what it cost you.

Jewelry

Jewelry is the traditional way for lower-income people to own a little bit of gold. The dual-use nature of jewelry lets them buy a gift and make an investment at the same time. This is very true in third-world countries, and a big part of the culture in India and China. It is a way to have an asset in a country that generally discourages that or periodically confiscates it all. Not even the most stupid dictators would try to take a womans wedding rings!! But you can only wear so much at a time, or you end up looking like a Calcutta hooker or LA pimp daddy. So its good in small amounts, but not larger. And you have a big difference between price and melt value, so as an investment it doesn't really work. If you disagree, go buy some jewelry and take it immediate to a "cash for gold" place to see what they will pay you.

Other Comments

Confiscation is a concern for a lot of people. The US government did it in 1933, and this president seems to worship FDR. I have always thought it was over-the-top to think they could do it again. But some really smart people think it is inevitable, so I have to seriously consider it. One scenario has the government requiring all citizens to redeem their gold for cash. Likely they will pay you at (or even above) market rates. Once they have all the gold in their possession, they can take the USA off the floating exchange rate system, declare gold to be worth $20,000 an ounce, and they are back in business with a gold-based dollar (albeit one that is devastated in terms of purchasing power).

The legal way to avoid having your gold confiscated is to get it out of the country ahead of time. If you live near the northern border, take a ride to Canada and open a safe deposit box. If you have a home in another country, store it there. You can also open a depository account or a gold based account in many countries. There are two types. With one (unallocated), you have a part-ownership in a generic pool of physical gold. But you can also have what they call an allocated account, where you have ownership of specific gold coins or bars. An allocated account is more expensive, but there is no risk at all. With an unallocated account, it is conceivable that if the depository institution goes bankrupt you may be part of the general creditors and waiting in line for your payout. You need to pick your institution carefully.

Your other alternative is to have physical possession of your gold, not in a safe deposit box. You can bury it in the backyard or hide it in your sock drawer and just wait out the prohibition on gold ownership. The last time they did it, it lasted 40 years.

My own take is that complete confiscation seems less likely than in the past. Last time they exempted collectible coins, and that is a lot fuzzier line this time. Is a proof coin collectible? How about foreign coins like Pandas? If a coin has been graded by a coin grading service, most anyone would consider it to be collectible. Of course they could try to get the collectible coins as well, since the government can and will do anything they can get away with. In my mind, the most likely outcome is that they nationalize the ETF's. Why spend a lot of time going after coins one at a time when the GLD ETF has 10,000 tons of gold in it's possession? They could almost double official reserves in one swoop, without getting out their guns. They just pay off shareholders at market (which is ultimately all an ETF owner can expect anyway), collect their taxes, and move on.

More on Bullion

So as you can see, for that SHTF money, physical bullion that you can hold in your hands is the superior investment for most people. You have several options for buying gold and silver bullion.

Preservation of Wealth

Preservation of Wealth (POW) is a buying club, with wholesale prices available to their members. Current pricing is $52 over spot for an American Eagle. They also sometimes have member specials as low as $25 over spot. You can buy a single coin or a thousand. In the interest of full disclosure, once you are a member you can earn a referral for each member that you refer. Refer just a couple of people and your membership is free. Look over the details and join if you see how it makes sense. Once you become a member, share your own link with your friends and earn the referrals for them. If you refer a lot of people, you might even make some real money. Use it to buy more coins. LOL.

Tulving.com

There are several national dealers that have very good pricing. One of the biggest in Tulving.com They always have the most competitive prices for both buying and selling, and list their premiums over spot right on their website. But you have to be a quantity buyer. That means a minimum of 500 ounces of silver or 20 ounces of gold at one time and of a single type. No mix and match. If you want big quantities at one time, these are the guys to check out. Yet POW has the same pricing (sometimes cheaper) without the minimums. The difference is POW has an annual membership fee. Check the Tulving website, then call POW for a fair comparison.

Traditional Dealer

There are two groups. National dealers and local dealers. But essentially the same rules apply. Prices will vary a lot from dealer to dealer, and sometimes from day to day. Today's price may be $75 over spot or $125 over spot, but that changes at the whim of the dealer, possibly based on their inventory or their cost basis or if the rent is due. You have to do lots of price research if you want to buy from them, and do the same research every time. The other issue encountered is that when prices drop, small dealers are mysteriously out-of-stock, and you just can't buy bullion at good prices. It can be extremely frustrating to have a buying plan in place, have prices drop to your target, only to have dealers lock up their inventory while they await higher prices. This caused me to miss a great buying opportunity when gold was at $700$750 in 2008. It is why I went on the hunt to find Tulving (and now POW). This issue is not a problem at Tulving or POW. They just ride the market wherever it goes and keep on selling.

Local Classifieds / Craigs List

This is NOT a reliable source of coins, but you may get lucky. Your goal in buying or selling here is to take out the middleman (dealer) and split the difference with the other party. So let's say a gold eagle has a $20 spread between market buy and sell prices. You can save $10 an ounce by seeking out these people. Or you may get even better prices if you are dealing with an unknowledgeable seller and you can convince them your lower price is a good one. Or you may find someone who wants to sell for cash and does not want a paperwork trail. The new health insurance law requires dealers to issue a 1099 for basically anything they purchase, so someone trying to avoid taxes may give you a nice deal. If you run an ad looking to buy gold, people will call you with all kinds of oddball things including private mint medallions, plated souvenir coins, and clads. You have to be very careful of fakes. They will usually think their oddball coins or fakes are worth way more than reality. You may find yourself driving around town and meeting strangers with a lot of cash in your car. Be security-conscious. I don't have an opinion about any of this. Just be knowledgeable whatever you decide.

CHAPTER 3:
GOLD AND SILVER BUYING MISTAKES

Detailed below are the most common pitfalls that precious metals investors often encounter.

Common Mistake #1 - Unrealistic Expectations

One of the biggest pitfalls faced by precious metal investors of all experience levels is impatience and the temptation to chase the price with the hopes of "hitting it big". Many new investors believe that the metals prices can only go up and that investing success is a given in the short term.

The key to success is the full understanding that investing in gold or silver is a long-term proposition. You can only measure your success over many YEARS, not weeks or even months. If you are looking to "get rich quick" we would recommend you not venture in to precious metals with this expectation.

Take the time to assess the following:

What are your investment goals?

Why are you considering gold and silver?

Will the factors that are moving you to consider precious metals change in the near future?

Most likely you are considering precious metals due to a myriad of global economic conditions - most of which will not change quickly, if at all. This only reinforces a long-term position and mentality when it comes to investing in metals. If you get in the game, do so for the long haul.

Keep in mind the flip side as well. Investors will often jump from investment vehicle to vehicle if their investment strategy doesn't yield immediate results. We have see many of our clients sell off their metals to go and invest in the "next big thing", have it fail and then find themselves buying metals back at significantly higher prices.

Common Mistake #2 - Chasing the Price

Some people will spend years chasing after the next big thing, often believing that this strategy is "the one." When that particular strategy doesn't yield the results they were looking for, the common response by investors is to blame the strategy and to quickly adopt another. They don't realize that the problem most often lies within themselves and not with a given strategy or tactic.

Again, step back...

Give the strategy some time. We can't stress enough that precious metals investments should be long-term holdings. Success in this game is not something that can be accurately measured in weeks or months. This is a long-term commitment. Budget your time, energy and capital wisely.

Common Mistake #3 - ETF's and Physical Metals are the Same Many investors, especially those new to precious metals, make the critical error of thinking that owning an Exchange Traded Fund (ETF) that invests in gold, such as GLD, is the same as owning the physical gold itself. It is critical to understand the key differences between owning shares of an ETF and owning physical gold or silver.

For thousands of years, physical gold and silver have been highly desirable and recognizable commodities that are easily bought, sold and exchanged for goods on local and world markets. You can take physical gold from New York to Zimbabwe and everyone will immediately recognize the inherent value in the metal itself. In essence, you can use physical gold or silver in lieu of, or for exchange of cash all over the world.

As the owner of a gold ETF, you ultimately only own a piece of paper, a promissory note, showing how many shares of the fund you own; however you do not own any actual physical gold. The ETF owns the gold and you own a promise from the fund managers to pay back the value of the shares you have purchased in the ETF. The ETF certificate that you own is something that is not universally traded on the world markets, nor is it widely recognized or easily exchangeable for currency. You would have a very difficult time trying to trade paper certificates for goods or services the same way you would physical gold.

Let's take a closer look at one of the most popular gold investments, GLD. The primary disadvantage of paper gold is lack-of-ease in converting to physical gold. While investors may own a claim on physical gold, in many cases they will find that actually getting their hands on the metal is much more difficult than they had expected.

Investors may not realize that when they invest in GLD, they do not own physical gold. Yes, in theory GLD is a physical gold-backed ETF, and one share of GLD is supposed to be equivalent to 1/10th ounce of gold. But the actual story is much more complicated, with major restrictions on redemption.

First, to qualify to redeem GLD shares for physical gold, special permission is required from the trustee of GLD. This permission is typically reserved for brokers and major institutional players. Second, shares can only be redeemed in batches of 100,000, which equates to roughly $13 million at today's prices. Third, according to GLD's prospectus, the fund retains the right to settle gold requests in cash rather than in the physical metal. So even if you owned 100,000 shares and had permission to redeem them, you still might not receive your physical bullion.

Another nuance to investing in GLD has to do with how its price moves in relation to the spot price of gold on the futures market. While the initial price of GLD was set to represent the price of 1/10th ounce of gold, this relationship has not been maintained, because GLD is subject to its own market forces, as well as reduction in value through management fees. Without getting into too much detail, the price of GLD is highly correlated with the spot price movements of gold, but does not follow those movements exactly. For example, a large purchase or sale of shares in GLD can drive the price up or down, without the spot price of gold changing.

Finally, if you read the language of an ETF prospectus carefully, you will see that your investment in the ETF could possibly drop to $0 in value. This highlights two critical factors to consider about ETFs: 1) you are trusting someone else to establish the value of the gold possessed by the ETF, and 2) you are trusting that the fund managers actually have enough physical gold to cover your investment and all of the other shares invested as well.

These two concerns are negated when you consider physically possessing gold. First, the value of your investment is determined by the market, not by a fund manager or by the popularity of the shares of a given ETF. Second, since you physically possess the gold, you know exactly what it is worth at any moment in time and are not dependent on another person or entity to tell you what you have.

The chance of physical gold becoming worthless is virtually impossible, given that gold and silver have always had, and should always have value. While the value of gold may fluctuate depending on a given currency or during any given day, there will always be some value associated with these precious metals due to the fact that precious metals are rare elements, cannot be "manufactured" and have a myriad of industrial uses.

Common Mistake #4 - Falling for Confiscation Scare Tactics

Countless investors have been presented with the "Confiscation Myth" and unknowingly found themselves being upsold into unnecessary, expensive numismatic coins. Many unscrupulous precious metals firms will bait investors in to buying numismatic coins that have a margin that is 28 to 70% higher than standard bullion coins and bars.

The most frequently used technique to promote high-priced coins is to raise the issue of confiscation. Many telemarketers tell investors that old U.S. gold coins are not "subject to confiscation," leaving the impression that modern gold bullion coins are. Consequently, many investors buy old, rare, and antique gold coins at prices significantly higher than the value of their gold content. The idea of buying "nonconfiscatable" gold sounds like a powerful argument but when scrutinized fails to stand the test of truth.

Many precious metals firms maintain that old U.S. gold coins, proof sets, and commemorative gold coins are "collectibles" and would not be subject to another gold recall. Some firms say that premiums of at least 15% automatically make coins collectibles. Another notion holds that coins one hundred years or older are antiques and therefore not subject to confiscation.

The bottom line is that NO federal law or Treasury department regulation supports these contentions.

ONLY if you are a collector or speculator should you buy numismatic coins.

Common Mistake #5 - Minimal Research

When faced with something new, it's easy to simply take the advice of a few friends or scan a couple of websites before you make the jump. In the precious metals market, superficial research is just looking at general information such as spot prices and trying to "pick a price point" or choosing the most popular forms to buy. There is significant information to be learned about buying gold and silver, and that requires sifting through the misinformation as well.

There are sound forums and blogs to review such as zerohedge.com, seekingalpha.com, cointalk.com and goldismoney.com. They are great places to read other investors' opinions, strategies and the experiences they've had with specific dealers. Ask specific questions on the forums and mine the resources and experience of seasoned investors.

You can also turn to Facebook and LinkedIn for various investor groups and interest groups. Please keep in mind that many of these groups are formed by dealers or individuals that have a hidden sales agenda. Consider their profile and background before considering any aspect of investment advice that is offered.

There are a number of industry respected company blogs that are hosted by dealers and wholesalers that are another solid source of information for a new or experienced investor. Many of the industry blogs provide new product information, Mint news and up to date market information.

The mainstream media will often provide timely, yet sometimes biased news. Use your discernment when reviewing precious metals news from The Wall Street Journal, TheStreet.com, YahooFinance or Reuters. Verify any news you read with multiple reliable sources.

In the end after your initial research, find a dealer that is willing to spend time answering any and all of your questions without trying to sell you something.

Common Mistake #6 - Going "All In"

Many first-time precious metal investors make the mistake of investing all or a significant portion of their savings in precious metals. That is a mistake! You should never invest all or a significant portion of your assets in any single investment vehicle. To determine how much you should invest, you must first determine how much you can actually afford to invest and what your financial goals are.

When you determine how much to invest in precious metals you should begin by following some long-standing investment principles. If you have significant debt, you should work first to pay down your debt and secure three to six months of living expenses in savings. If these principles are accomplished then take a look to see how much additional savings you have on hand for investing.

Follow this with a plan to add to your investments over time. You should plan to use a specified portion of your income to build your precious metal portfolio over time. This method is called "dollar-cost-averaging" and it is useful whether buying stocks, bonds, mutual funds, precious metals or any investment. Speak with a qualified financial advisor to set up a budget and determine how much of your future income you should invest.

For many types of investments, a minimum initial investment amount may be required. Different precious metals dealers require different minimum purchases. Your local dealer may let you buy just one or two ounces of silver, while some online dealers require upwards of $5,000 to purchase from them. We, for example, do not have a minimum purchase requirement.

Finally, never borrow money to invest, never buy precious metals on leverage and don't use money set aside for other needs.

Common Mistake #7 - Obsession

Did you know that a Google search for the word "gold" produces over 700,000,000 results? "Silver" brings back about 480,000,000 results. That is some serious information overload and way too much for any one person to try to keep up with.

Many newcomers to precious metals investing may find that they become overwhelmed with information, especially when gold fever hits or when the price reaches a new all-time high. There is so much to learn and so many things happening all at once all over the world, it's easy to catch the fever and want to keep constant vigil over the market. This gives new investors a misguided sense of control, thinking that as long as they are keeping an eye on the market, they'll be on top of things.

Right? In reality, the opposite is happening.

The Sun is always shining somewhere on the Earth, and there is a market somewhere that is almost always open - this is especially apparent with today's Internet connected markets and global economies. Markets constantly change based on events all around the world - there's just no way for any one person to keep up with the precious metals market 24/7.

The solution?

Relax. Don't become obsessed with the ever-changing world of precious metals - give your mind a break from it all. When our brains are strained, we tend to make high-risk decisions with a lack of concern for the consequences. It'll still be there when you return. If you have done your homework, work with a reputable company to place your orders and have a solid long-term strategy in place, you will hardly miss a beat.

One way to ensure you are using a great strategy is to pre-plan your moves - be less reactive and more proactive. This gives a real sense of control and allows you to calculate your strategy and wait for the best timing. The markets move as they will, so instead of reacting to everything, which requires you to watch the Hong Kong Market to guess what will happen in London, you can pre-plan your moves.

Investing in precious metals is serious business but it can be very rewarding. This type of endeavor requires both attention and respect. Master it and a world of financial opportunity is open to you. Fall victim to it and there are few things more frustrating. Hopefully, from this short report you have gained a better awareness of the rapidly changing and in-depth nature of precious metals and how to maximize your opportunity to succeed.

The pitfalls we have illustrated here are just some of the more common mistakes that new investors experience. You can avoid the headache of these blunders by keeping in mind some of the crucial information we have revealed in this report. Above all, remember that success will be measured in years, not weeks. Avoid the mindset of getting rich quick - keep your goals and expectations long term.

Also, remember that there is no substitute for knowledge and practice. Educate yourself. Find a system that makes sense to you. Don't go along with something simply because you were told it works. Rather, determine what resonates with your own body of knowledge and experience, then stick with your strategy.

Finally, find a mentor - someone who is willing to impart the knowledge that made them successful. A solid understanding of precious metals investing is truly invaluable, offering you the opportunity for secure investments, financial strength and independence.

SIMPLE AND SAFE STEPS INVESTING IN GOLD AND SILVER

Tip 1. People globally are accumulating gold & silver to protect against the debt crisis.

An increasing number of individuals and investors globally are buying gold & silver in the first place to protect their wealth and savings. Even Central banks are accumulating gold on a large scale. What can we learn from this trend? People are protecting their purchasing power against the negative effects of the ongoing global debt crisis. Gold and silver are a safe store of value. With one ounce of gold you will be able to buy the same goods in let's say 3 years. The paper money you are owning will lose its value over the same period of time.

We are witnessing a severe crisis, caused by excessive amounts of government debts and massive money printing mainly in the Western countries and Japan. The most logic outcome of those practices is inflation, which results in a declining value of paper money.

Tip 2. You too should own gold & silver, it's very simple. It became very simple over the past years to own precious metals. There are actually more ways than ever to buy gold & silver. Here are some
tips:

- Ideally you buy gold and silver in the form of 100g bars, 250g bars or 500g bars. Don't buy large bars, as you will potentially encounter difficulties selling them. Make sure you own the metal; so an unallocated solution from your bank is not an advised solution. A simple but safe solution is to store the metals in a personal safe, but not at home.

- Consider buying some gold and silver coins like the South African Kruegerrand, the Australian Kangaroo, the Swiss Vreneli, the Canadian Maple Leaf or the American Eagle. Don't buy exotic coins as you will have difficulties to find buyers when you want to sell.

- There are Exchange Traded Funds (ETF's) you can buy on the stock exchanges. Make sure you only buy the ETF's that are backed with physical gold and silver, like Sprott Physical Trust or Central Fund of Canada.

- You can easily buy and store precious metals via online programs. The huge advantage is that the metal is stored in a safe vault, which is usually included in the service. We like BullionVault.com and GoldMoney.com. For US and Canadian citizens, there is an accessible silver savings program SilverSaver.com. If you prefer Swiss authenticity 100% outside the banking system, then you should consider GlobalGold.ch.

Tip 3. Be sure to own physical gold & silver, avoid paper holdings.

Avoid as much as possible buying paper gold or silver, like the ETF's GLD and SLV. They became very popular because of their ease of use, but there are some risks associated with the ETF's. As a general rule of thumb, remember to own your gold and silver outside the banking system. We're afraid that ETF's could be knocked down when a systemic financial crisis should occur. If you want an example of what can go wrong with paper gold, then have a look at the recent drama that occurred with MF Global: investors simply lost all their money.

Tip 4. We are in stage 2 of the 3 in the gold bull market, still far away from the top.

Every market goes from undervalued to fairly valued and finally overvalued. These are long term trends which are called "wealth cycles". The key to be successful in your personal or professional investment life, is to get rid of overvalued assets in order to accumulate undervalued assets.

If you look at the current gold and silver prices, you might think that the metals are overvalued. You could be wrong. Expressed in nominal terms, the prices look high indeed. But if you monitor following indicators, you'll get another picture:

- When taking inflation into account, the gold and silver price are much lower than their peak of 1980.
- When looking at the personal ownership of gold and silver, you'll see a ratio of roughly 1:10.000 people in the Western world who own the metal.
- When comparing the current gold and silver investments with the ones at the top of the previous bull market in 1980, you'll see a ridiculous low amount of invested assets in precious metals today.

- We did not see any parabolic move of the gold or silver price. If you look back to 1980, you'll see what parabolic means.

We are currently in the second stage of the bull market. When we enter the third and final stage, a hype will occur and everybody will rush to own gold and silver. Clearly "smart money" is already profiting from the current undervaluation of gold and silver; as usual, they are ahead of the herd. Are you too?

Tip 5. Be prepared to see serious price moves, mainly in silver... it's normal.
In general, all commodity markets tend to move sharply. Gold and especially silver follow the same principle. It's quite common to see the silver price move 3% or more on a particular day. As the long term bull market in gold & silver continues, the volatility intensifies as well. So we can expect an even more intense price action. Be prepared and do not panic, it's a characteristic of the bull market.

The "heart fainted" investor will preferably need to focus on gold. If you are not afraid of volatility and you have an iron stomach, then you could go for silver. You'll have potentially higher profits. But be sure to time your purchase.

Tip 6. Timing your purchase is crucial, never chase prices higher.
One of the key decisions is to determine when to do your purchase. It's a decisions you should base on the long term charts. The "golden" rule is to buy the dips (they always come) and avoid buying at the peaks.

When you have a look at the gold chart of the past 10 years, you'll see that the price is moving perfectly in a range of higher highs and higher lows. Don't chase prices higher; just wait to buy the dips. Don't be afraid of waiting a bit if prices are near an intermediate peak. You should welcome decreasing prices for the buying opportunity you get.

Tip 7. The previous century was for gold, this one is for silver.
During the past decade both gold and silver performed very well in nominal terms. When looking at the gold/silver ratio, most precious metals experts agree that the silver price will increase sharper than gold. One of the reasons is that the historical gold/silver ratio is

approximately 16/1. The ratio tends to move to that average on a longer term basis. Currently it's almost 60. Do you see the opportunity?

Another way to estimate the potential of a silver investment, is to look at the supply side. Silver is expected to encounter severe shortages because of the combination of its increasing industrial usage and increasing investment demand. You would be surprised to learn how much industries are using silver as a raw material in manufacturing products. Silver is all around you: your laptop, mobile phone, jewels, light switch, your car, mirrors, solar panels, batteries, electrical products like TV or washing machine, etc.

CHAPTER 4

Understanding the Gold Silver Ratio and How to SwapSwapping the Gold/Silver Ratio - Seeking a 15 - 35% Return With No Cash Outlay

The upward trend in the metals has many investors owning both. But, there's more you can do with gold and silver bullion than just buy and hold. You can also periodically trade, or "swap", one for the other. To do so successfully, you first need to understand the gold/silver ratio.

The gold/silver ratio tells you the number of ounces of silver it would take to purchase one ounce of gold at a specific time. If you examine gold and silver prices going back 4,000 years, will find:

- The historical ratio is 16:1 (it has taken 16 ounces of silver to buy 1 ounce of gold)
- For the last 100 years, the ratio has been 30:1
- In the last 12 years, the ratio has held closer to 60:1
- In just the past the past 5 years, the ratio has fluctuated from the low 40's to almost 100

- As of March 1st, 2011, the gold/silver ratio was sitting slightly below 40:1

How do we take advantage of this fluctuation?
- First - we time our purchases based on the ratio. When the ratio is relatively high, we favor silver in new purchases. When the ratio is relatively low, we favor gold.
- Last - we act when the ratio reaches tops and bottoms. When the ratio is high, we swap gold for silver. Then when the ratio drops, we swap silver back into gold. Said another way, we swap silver for gold when silver has appreciated faster than gold. Then, we swap gold back into silver when silver becomes "cheap" relative to gold. Every time we go through this cycle - gold to silver and back to gold - we increase our ounces. That's the whole objective. For example:
- Suppose you had one ounce of gold, and the gold/silver ratio rose to 80:1. You would swap your one ounce of gold for 80 ounces of silver. When the ratio contracted to 40:1, you would swap your 80 ounces of silver back for 2 ounces of gold, doubling the number of ounces you hold.

- Next - we buy the form of silver or gold that offers the possibility of greater profits. During periods of high demand, investors will often bid up the premium on certain items 20 to 40% or more of their underlying value. At that point, we can swap the high premium items for others with lower premiums - capturing much of the difference, and converting that difference into extra ounces of metal.

Plus, utilizing this technique does not require any additional monetary outlay. Taking advantage of this ratio strategy beats the alternative - sitting still waiting for the price to rise.

CAUTIONS

- Taxes - If you realize a profit from the transaction, you may owe tax on the gain. We do not offer tax advice. Please consult your tax specialist.
- Market risk - I do not determine swapping price points independently. Rather, I lean heavily on others in the industry that have also been practicing technique for decades. The market may not cooperate. The challenge is correctly identifying the swapping points based on the relative valuations between the metals. The ratio might move much

higher or lower than our target. We would then need to wait longer for the ratio to readjust itself. This is the essential risk to those trading the ratio.

- Costs - Transaction costs such as shipping, the bid-ask price spread and commission can reach as much as 8%, although they should be lower. We will need to hold the trade long enough to recoup the transaction costs. Transaction costs associated with trading physical metals are higher than trading ETF's, futures or other paper instruments. In order to keep your costs low, we charge only one-half of our normal commission for a swap transaction. Many others will charge a full commission on both the buy and the sell side. Be careful.

BENEFITS

☐ More Ounces at no cost - The Gold/Silver ratio trading strategy takes an investment that is otherwise stagnant and creates growth by increasing the number of ounces you hold - with no additional cash outlay. Between now and the end of the bull market you should conservatively expect to double your ounces utilizing this strategy.

What You Need to Know

When I first started to buy metals almost 20 years ago, my mentor frequently reminded me that he was not a prophet. In the same vein, if I am wrong about gold/silver ratio, it will cost you money. You'll buy silver instead of gold and the gold will outpace the silver, or vice versa. I don't think that will happen. Or, if it does, it will be temporary. Sometimes the time-frame between swaps is relatively short - maybe only a few months. Other times it has taken two years or longer.

I am recommending swapping silver for gold when the gold/silver ratio drops to 48 or less. Consider swapping more if the ratio drops further. We will then seek the opportunity to swap that gold back into silver, capturing that gain in additional ounces of silver.

Because there are commissions and other transaction costs, you will not realize exactly the same ratio as the spot ratio.

The swapping strategy works for both small and large investors as long as you are willing to swap (150) ounces of silver or more. We will swap into the lowest cost, most readily available, most liquid gold coins - whatever offers you the most gold for your silver.

This is not a solicitation, only a strategy. Please do your own due diligence and make your own investment decision.

I still ultimately favor silver over gold as I remain convinced that the ratio will reach 16:1 (or lower) at the top of this bull market.

Housekeeping

It is impossible to swap an exact amount of one metal for the exact amount of another. For example, one ounce of gold might buy 50.17 ounces of silver, but never exactly 50 ounces even. I do my very best to swap as close to even-up as possible. The residual we will settle in cash. You may owe a small amount, or you may be due a small amount. I attempt to keep these amounts under $100.

The gold/silver swapping opportunity is presenting itself intermittently.

If you are interested in learning more on how you might increase your metal holdings by 15 to 35% or more, with no cash outlay, please contact us. The window of opportunity is very narrow.

Why Silver Is a Better Investment Than Gold

1. The historic silver/gold price ratio was 16:1, but in recent years, silver is relatively cheaper ranging from about 40:1 to 80:1. On October 12, 2009, with silver at $17.75/oz. and gold at $1,057/oz., the ratio is 60:1. This means that silver is currently undervalued, and cheaper than historic norms, and thus it is a better investment than even gold if you want to "buy low and sell high".

2. The supply and demand fundamentals for silver are extraordinary. There has been an ongoing supply/demand deficit in silver for 12 years. More silver is consumed by industry than is produced by mining and recycling combined. Some say this deficit reaches back 60 years, and has consumed virtually all the known silver ever mined since the beginning of the world. The annual deficit has recently ranged from 100 million to 200 million ounces per year. Annual supply is about 650 million ounces, and annual demand is about 800 million ounces.

3. Considering refined and mined known silver reserves, there is far less silver in the world than gold.

Approximately 150 million ounces of silver vs. 4 billion ounces of gold.

4. Most silver, 70-80% brought to market, is mined as a by-product of copper mining, gold mining, or zinc and lead mining. There are very few primary silver mines in the world, since most are really copper or gold mines. Therefore, mild increases in the price of silver will not bring substantially more silver out of the ground. Much silver is consumed in photography; electronics, medicine and numerous other industries. There is so little silver used in any one application (cell phone, photograph, electric terminal), that price increases in silver will probably not reduce demand. With a relatively inelastic supply, and relatively inelastic demand, it will require a dramatic explosion in price to bring the supply and demand deficit back into balance.

5. Famous investors have bought silver in recent years. In 1997, Warren Buffet bought 130 million ounces of real silver, due to the favorable "supply and demand fundamentals", he bought as much as they would let him legally buy, yet his purchase was with about 2% of the value of his portfolio. George Soros owns a large

percentage of Apex Silver (SIL). Bill Gates owns a substantial position in Pan American Silver (PAAS).

6. In the gold market, there has been a large increase in paper futures contracts which are used to suppress the price. In silver, the relative amount of paper contracts is much larger. In other words, there are more paper shorts that will be caught in an impossible situation when the price of silver really begins to rise due to the fundamental supply demand gap. They will be forced to buy silver or go bankrupt. Either action will cause a dramatic rise in the silver price. If they default on the silver contracts, that will signal to the world the severe shortage of silver, and signal a great investment opportunity.

7. One of the cheapest ways to buy silver: You can buy U.S. coins dated 1964 or earlier, $1000 face value (4,000 quarters, or 2,000 half dollars, or 10,000 dimes), in a "bag" of "junk silver", which contain 715-720 ounces of silver, depending on how worn the coins are. In the early 1980's, when silver was $30-$50/oz., a bag of silver could be used to buy a house! We could see that day again - soon!

8. But historically, a silver dime was a day's wage, whether 100 years ago, or in Roman times when a denarius was a day's wage. This means that a dime of silver, worth $1.27 today, could be worth over $150 (which is a day's wage in today's money.) or more, now that silver is scarce. Actually, in 1926, a silver dime could pay the rent at a 5 star hotel for a month! That's worth about $6000 to $10,000!

You get so much silver for your money. A bag of junk silver weighs about 55 pounds, and is the size of a bowling ball. If you invested $100,000 into junk silver coins, at $12,450/bag, that would give you 8 bags each weighing 55 pounds, or about 440 pounds total. Could you imagine moving that much around your house if you had to move? Silver is so cheap it creates physical problems for investors today!

You will sometimes find quarters in a bag dating back to the late 1800's. In the early 1900's, you could work ALL DAY for a wage of ONE SILVER QUARTER. Imagine being able to buy a day's wage of real money for less than a dollar of today's money! Today, in 2009, a day's wage is over $100. Another way to put it is that the dollar has lost over 99% of its purchasing power over time. Yet, due to silver being undervalued, you can get 100 times the value of your money and labor if you invest in silver. Imagine if they paid a day's wage today of $100 in silver quarters; they would have to give you about 100 silver quarters today. The implications are that if silver returns to its historic valuations, silver will need to go up in value about 100 times, to $450/oz. Silver is truly a bargain.

At the risk of sounding like a conspiracy theorist, the silver price has been manipulated and kept artificially low for years. The United States used to have the largest strategic stockpile in the world - in excess of 3 billion ounces. Today we hold essentially zero. Today, some reports put the amount of available silver on the COMEX at 60 million ounces. (The COMEX stands for the Commodity Exchange, which is a division of the NYMEX - New York Mercantile Exchange. This is where precious metals futures contracts are traded).

This presents an investment opportunity of a lifetime. Actually, it is more likely that silver today is the greatest investment opportunity in the history of the world.

* Never before in human history, has the entire world left using silver as money.

* Never before in human history, has the entire world consumed nearly all the silver for use in electronics.

* Never before in human history, has silver become so cheaply valued.

* Soon, never before in human history have we virtually run out of available above-ground silver.

Silver is a steal! It's cheap - too cheap!

All of them share growing concerns and anxiety regarding the state of our economy and the fiscal and monetary policy of our government.
Many people are considering safe haven investments.

Especially during this time of economic uncertainty, there are numerous individuals and organizations "pushing" gold and silver. They are often recommending items with the highest profit margins, without regard to the Gold: Silver ratio, while attempting to "up-sell" and promote specific inventory that may not be the best for you, the investor. As a result, you end up paying "full retail" with an additional 5% to 20% in unnecessary commissions.

CHAPTER 5
GOLD VS SILVER

A Revolution is defined as "a turn around" or fundamental change in power that takes place in a relatively short period of time. There is a Silver Revolution going on worldwide, yet mainstream media, particularly in the U.S., has failed to report about it. The U.S. has gone from being net sellers of silver, to recently becoming buyers of the precious metal and the trend is gaining international momentum-causing the purchasing power of silver to increase dramatically. Within the last 10 years the price of silver has quadrupled, and since February 2010, silver has increased by 30%, outpacing gold's rise of 17%. Despite the fact that nearly every American consumes silver daily, less than 5% of us are actual saving and investing in the precious metal. This was not the case 50 years ago when it was common to carry pocket change made of 90% silver coins. Yet today, pre-1964 silver coins have become increasingly harder to find.

Many were melt down to silver bullion in 1980 when the price of silver soared to $50 per ounce. Peter Schiff, a

Financial forecaster with a track record of being "right", suggest that current conditions in the market are positioning both silver and gold to reach monumental surges in demand followed by worldwide shortages in supply that will drive silver to exceed the 1980 high. For the last 20 years the demand for silver has outstripped the diminishing supply. Silver miners and recyclers have been unable to meet the yearly demand so the government has made up for the deficit by depleting their own stockpile. According to U.S. Geologist, silver will be the first element on their periodic table to become extinct. Geologist estimate that we could run out of aboveground silver within a decade, by the year 2020. This would make it increasing more expensive to mine the limited under-ground reserve, while it also guarantees the future price of silver will rise tremendously due to lack of supply and growing demand. Silver is irreplaceable due to the abundance of industrial uses in everything from mirrors, electric conductors, solar panels, batteries, technology, cell phones, photography, dentistry, electronics and computers--to coins, silverware and jewelry. In addition, silver compounds (Ag) kill bacteria in external wounds and create life saving medicines, antibiotics and disinfectants. The world as we know it today can not exist without silver. Yet few are aware of the scarcity and rarity of this truly precious metal.

GROWING INVESTMENT DEMAND

Although silver has immeasurable uses, it's the growing demand for silver as an Investment that has intensified immensely across the globe. For the first time ever, China has launched an ad campaign encouraging citizens to purchase silver bullion for investment, making it readily available for sale at local banks. India bought 200 metric tons of gold to diversify out-of-the-dollar and is buying silver for both industrial use and as an Investment. Meanwhile, the U.S. is experiencing difficulty keeping up with the continued, sustained demand for American Silver Eagle Proof coins and has suspended production. Canada is experiencing similar dilemma's.

Silver, aka "the poor mans gold" is extremely undervalued and affordable at under $20 per ounce, compared to gold which hovers at over $1200 per ounce. Unlike silver which is consumed, gold is hoard. Therefore most of the gold ever mined in the world within the last 5000 years is recycled and stored in vaults at central banks. They are notorious for hoarding the gold then selling it back into the market place to depress the price. Gold has no industrial or medical value and is solely used as a storage of wealth. The price of gold is currently at an all time high and is also positioned to rise a good deal higher. In contrast, the low price point of silver make it more accessible to the average person who can gain substantial returns on their investment while also protecting their purchasing power. The affordability factor is one of the main reasons people around the world are gaining entry into this exclusive market. These days silver is not simply for the "poor man", the rich are also investing in silver! Jim Rodgers, an American Investor who made his first millions buying low and selling high, BUYS silver because it's 60-70% below it's all time high and is much more depressed in price than gold or any other precious metal. Warren Buffet, the largest silver Investor ever, bought 130 million ounces of silver in 1997-98 and is rumored to have sold it to the Silver Exchange Traded Fund (SLV) in 2006.

As the currency crisis worsens worldwide, more people are becoming aware of the history of fiat currencies and how they have all completely failed over time. As seen in the U.S. in 1781 when the Continental currency collapsed and ceased to circulate as money and most recently in 2008 when the Zimbabwean currency collapsed. Black market trading in precious metals was common practice before the Zimbabwean dollar was replaced with foreign currencies. The economies of Portugal, Italy, Ireland, Greece and Spain (PIIGS) are especially at risk due to increasingly high levels of government debt and deficits relative to annual GDP. This has resulted a credit rating downgrade, devaluation of currency and chaos in the streets. A revolution is well underway in Greece as citizens galvanize to protest the government's pay freeze and taxing the middle working class people who refuse to pay government debts ($53 billion euros) out of their own pocket. Some Economist predict the future of the U.S. will be the same.

Rising U.S. DEBT

For first time in history on June 3, 2010, the US National debt clock reached a staggering $13 Trillion dollars and has no end in site--just more spending on unfunded liabilities, stimulus packages and bailouts in the Trillions. It's hard to comprehend the amount of $1 Trillion dollars, let alone 13 Trillion, but here's a note worthy perception. If President Bush could spend $1 million dollars a day from the day Jesus was born until now, he would only have spent about three quarters of a Trillion.

And if President Obama could spend $1 every second since the time human beings first starting using stone tools and fire, he'd have to spend money for over 412,000 years to get to $13 Trillion. This is chilling when you consider that fact that in 2000 President Clinton had the largest U.S. surplus ever of $230 billion dollars, with nine consecutive years of budget improvements. Yet, within the last 10 short years the U.S. has gone from hundreds of billions in surplus, to being the largest debtor nation in the world. Debt continues to rise at the most rapid pace in U.S. history. It's estimated to rise to 19.6 Trillion by 2015. This is simply unsustainable. Rapid increases in the money supply historically have caused inflation, leading to hyperinflation, followed by the return to hard money (silver and gold). When the circulating currency becomes excessively devalued, as what's happing with the U.S. dollar, economies revert to hard currencies and barter. The hard currency of choice will be one that the people can afford--silver. Which has outlasted all paper fiat-currencies.

THINK AHEAD

Although we have little control over government spending, we can make better informed decisions with knowledge and access to resources. Anyone with a basic understanding of economics and fiat currencies can grasp why the price of silver will explode. The best plan of action is to do just that--ACT by converting fiat currencies to real money (silver) that can not be created with the stroke of a pen or by powering up the printing press. There is a flight to sound money and as with any investment, time is of the essence. The lack of U.S. media coverage on the Silver Revolution can be your chance to capitalize off this small niche industry before the masses become aware of this rare investment opportunity. Even a minute fraction of the 6.8 billion people in the world becoming consciously aware of the growing demand for silver would cause a dramatically redistribution of wealth into the hands of owners of the physical metal. Other countries have been given a heads up and I think it's time for America to wake up! Get out the rat race, fiat-paper chase, slave-to-debt syndrome and protect yourself against reckless government spending and debasement of currency. Silver has increased in value over the last 10 years and continues to rise. Whereas the U.S. dollar has declined since 2006 and has perpetually plummeted for the last 100 years, losing over 95% of it's value. Together China and India (Chindia) make up 40% of the world's population with knowledge and access to Silver. While Mexico, 5 % of world's population, is fortunate to still hold silver in their coined currency. But what about the U.S.! Don't hold your breath waiting for mass media to shed light on this growing trend. Monopolized corporations with vested interests have ulterior motives for keeping the masses in the dark. It's up to you to do your due diligence, research and act. Either way the Silver Revolution is well underway whether you're on the boat or not. Your ability to maintain purchasing power will be critical during the inflationary environment a few short years ahead.

Savvy investors are refocusing their attention to precious metals such as silver, as a safe haven and hedge against currency debasement, inflation and uncertainly. It's only natural that we prepare for a flight to safety.

HISTORY ALWAYS REPEATS

When we study history and not propaganda it becomes evident that history always repeats. Just think. If history repeats itself we could see Silver rise 2,400%, as done in 1970-1980 when the price of Silver went from $1.50 per oz to $50 per oz, a 25-fold increase. The average price of Silver in 2001 was only $4. If Silver were to have another 25-fold increase, the result would be Silver rising to over $110 per ounce. Robert Kiyosaki and Michael Maloney authors of "Guide to Investing in Gold & Silver", predict that Silver could rise extraordinary to $1500 per ounce if history should repeat and Silver and gold equal the same amount of money needed to pay off U.S. National Debt, as in 1934 and 1980. The average price of Silver in 2010 is currently under $20 per ounce making silver the best bang-for-the-dollar this decade! In percentage terms silver will perform better than gold. The price of Silver will inevitable skyrocket and those that own the physical metal will be in the game. Those that don't will watch the spectacle from the sidelines. The best way to invest in this precious metal is to buy .999 Fine Silver coins, bars and bullion. Remember "If you can't hold it, you don't own it" so make sure you take physical possession of your silver. No exceptions.

THE TWENTY FIRST CENTURY - GOLD AND SILVER BULL MARKET

During the last great gold rush in the late 1970's, only investors from the United States and the better part of Western Europe were able to participate. That was because back then, most other nations did not allow physical ownership of gold as it was either illegal to own, not available for investment or not in public demand. Many of the world's countries including Russia, Eastern Europe, China and India, as well as all other Asian nations, South America and Mexico were incapable of participating at the time.

Back in the 1970's, basically we had generations of savers, So many of the people within Western Europe and America that might of actually had the chance to invest, either didn't or invested too late into the last phase of the precious metal market cycle, losing more than they gained. The investor mindset today, is much different from the 70's. Today there are no savers, as banks are not handing out any interest. Therefore, there is no fiscal incentive to allow banks to hold and use your money any longer. Many people are now privately investing instead.

Furthermore in today's demographic; the current market demand structure shows the entire world's population is now capable of placing their own trade orders. These trades can be executed over the phone with brokers, or even simpler, going online with a few mouse clicks to purchase investments or place trades through their own brokerage accounts. Today there are more and more people becoming billionaires throughout the world as well. These new billionaires have deep pockets capable of large-scale investments. Many countries now are producing new billionaires coming from Russia, China, India, Africa, Asia and South America. In many of these countries, investing has actually become a national sport.

The best news of all is that this time around, the entire world is chasing the same limited supply of gold and an even more limited supply of silver to invest in compared to the 1970's gold rush. There is only a finite quantity of gold above and below ground. There is physically even less silver available, above and below ground. Due to its high demand in industry, part of it is consumed, and therefore cannot be reclaimed.

The world is now into the second phase of this century's precious metals bull market. Now these new large-scale investors are bringing in money and buying large quantities of physical metals. The general public as a whole still doubts these investments. They discount them as un-worthy investments in general, apparently not viewing them as tool to hedge assets for an un-stable economy. Over the last 10 years the central banks of the west have concentrated on selling their gold reserves, while within the last few years all central banks from the east have been accumulating.

The European Union is having a hard time with everything unraveling at once. Greece is in chaos, Spain is almost there, others closely to follow. The ECB is going to be forced to continue monetizing debt just to keep the system alive a little longer. However the euro system itself is tanking and most likely doomed to failure. The attention on the euro has taken away from the serious problems facing the dollar. Which in truth, is in even worse fiscal shape. The US Government debts will never be repaid. Deficit spending and social programs will not stop, regardless who wins the presidency in November. The debt ultimately will be inflated away by the power of the politicians and the printing press of the Federal Reserve.

We're seeing global conditions with the Iranian oil embargo creating alternative ways to pay for the oil outside the global dollar system. They are now using gold or other national currencies from China, Japan and India specifically. The BRICS countries now want to create their own monetary system for payment outside the dollar and swift systems. The IMF and World Bank are supporting this. The loss of the dollar as the world's reserve currency hangs in the balance.

There are many people predicting either a deflationary collapse or all out hyperinflation ending with the destruction of the dollar to occur within the United States. This will exponentially progress globally, as the world is still so saturated in dollars. The timetable varies according to whom you're listening too, but everyone agrees no later than the end of this decade, if not sooner. As global conditions worsen, the market prices for gold and silver are only going to rapidly increase.

Consider all the factors previously mentioned, the sheer volume of new investment capital that will be entering this market alone will be enormous. Alone, this will drive up market prices to levels never imagined before. Predictions of greater than $1,000.00 per ounce for silver and over $20,000.00 per ounce on gold have previously been made by many. Could there be truth to any of these figures? It is up to you, to decide if there is any truth to these facts and if they could be a positive determining factor to accelerate prices to these levels or not.

The third phase of the precious metal bull market will be indicative to seeing values of these metals quickly going off the charts. Experts do predict you have time to act and invest while were still in the second phase of this market cycle. If you wait until the third phase starts, for you, it is going to be too late. Those who position themselves correctly on this bull market are going to witness the greatest wealth transfer of all time. Those who find themselves on the other side will not be so lucky.

Silver is today's gold, while both metals are now severely undervalued, the white metal is predicted to be the better investment. It will be a more risky investment, due to its industrial applications and greater affinity to market manipulations. However in the end, it's expected to yield higher percentages of returns from its original purchasing cost, compared to gold. The best news is, for those lower-income earners, silver is much easier and cheaper to get started investing in. Be prepared, by protecting you and your family's assets today, for tomorrow.

www.ingramcontent.com/pod-product-compliance
Lightning Source LLC
Chambersburg PA
CBHW020553220526
45463CB00006B/2294